Memoirs
of the
Miraculous

New Testament Spiritual Gift Teaching and Experiences

By Shawn Patrick Williams, D. D.

A wholly owned subsidary of **TBN**

Memoirs of the Miraculous

Trilogy Christian Publishers A Wholly Owned Subsidary of Trinity Broadcasting Network

2442 Michelle Drive Tustin, CA 92780

Manufactured in the United States of America

10 9 8 7 6 5 4 3 2 1

Library of Congress Cataloging-in-Publication Data is available.

ISBN: 978-1-68556-111-6

E-ISBN: 978-1-68556-112-3

Dedication

This book is dedicated to all those revivalists that want the fire of the Holy Spirit to operate in their lives but desire the order and balance of the New Testament Scriptures. You may "miss it" sometimes. You most likely won't get everything perfect, and odds are you will see many people make mistakes trying to swim in the rivers of revival. That's okay. Never stop pursuing Jesus Christ and all the spiritual gifts He wants to release through your life.

I have spent twenty years of my Christian life pursuing a revival culture. I have preached in denominations that believe a variety of theories: that the gifts of the Spirit have stopped, that they never stopped, that all should operate in them at the same time, that teach gifts in theory only, that are afraid of the gifts because they don't fully understand them, and that have had a pretty healthy balance on the topic. May you pursue the miraculous realm and experience the fire of the Holy Spirit as true revivalist.

Table of Contents

Foreword

Memoirs of the Miraculous is a book to be read, believed, and receive a deeper understanding of the miraculous realm, which many times is ignored or simply not believed as it should.

The book is loaded with stunning testimonies of people transformed by the living Word of God and the Holy Spirit. These engaging, practical, relatable personal stories about testimonies are spiritual arrows of victory and great weapons of warfare. Revelation 12:11, "And they overcame him by the blood of the Lamb, and by the word of their testimony; and they loved not their lives unto the death." There is power in your testimony.

Every single testimony is a pointer that the same can be reproduced in another person. Testimonies are not just a recount of what the Lord has done but an instrument to unlock the supernatural. Testimonies are pointers to our heritage as believers. "Thy testimonies have I taken as an heritage forever, for they are the rejoicing of my heart" (Psalm 119:111).

The words and actions of Warrior Nation International continue to encourage the body of Christ to be a good ground for the Holy Spirit to work His wondrous ways. I remain incredibly grateful and humbled by their continued efforts.

Over many years, I have personally been blessed beyond belief by the brotherhood of Dr. Patrick Shawn Williams and his dedication to upholding the lordship of Christ and the authority of Scripture.

The presence of God in Shawn's life today is seen in the divine truths and revelations he has received and shares with others. Because he is not ashamed of the gospel, this truth is impacting nations for Christ, who are desperate to experience the unlimited supernatural power of God. Luke 9:26, "For whosoever shall be ashamed of me and of my words, of him shall the Son of man be ashamed, when he shall come in his own glory, and in his Father's, and of the holy angels."

Shawn's book is an invitation to those who are hungry, open-minded, and ready to receive this unstoppable message about "love for one another, for God is love." After you read, study, share, and meditate on this revelation, you will be strengthened in the midst of persecution. God is looking for His people who will not stop believing.

—Pastor Forson Swanzy

Founder of Forson Swanzy Ministries & Elevate Now

"The abuse or misuse of the application of Gifts of the Spirit is no excuse for no use." (Anonymous)

Endorsements

"Shawn Patrick Williams' writings are some of the most prolific writings in the body of Christ this decade."

—Bishop Harold Ray

Redeemed Life Church, West Palm Beach, FL

"Warrior Nations is one of the leading 'last days' evangelistic ministries God is using to impact America and the nations."

—Dorothy Spaulding

Watchmen Broadcasting Network, Augusta, GA

Joel 2:28-32

And it shall come to pass afterward, that I will pour out my spirit upon all flesh; and your sons and your daughters shall prophesy, your old men shall dream dreams, your young men shall see visions. And also upon the servants and upon the handmaids in those days will I pour out my spirit. And I will shew wonders in the heavens and in the earth, blood, and fire, and pillars of smoke. The sun shall be turned into darkness, and the moon into blood, before the great and the terrible day of the LORD come. And it shall come to pass, that whosoever shall call on the name of the LORD shall be delivered: for in mount Zion and in Jerusalem shall be deliverance, as the LORD hath said, and in the remnant whom the LORD shall call.

Introduction

"Those things don't happen anymore. They're of the devil, and anyone you see or hear doing it, you should stay away from. They're wrong! We have everything we need from God, now in His Word, so there's no need of those things today. When all the apostles of the Lamb died, the gifts of the Spirit stopped." This is the answer I was told when, as an eight-year-old child, I asked about speaking in tongues to someone in the church that I grew up in. I had a friend whose family was from a Pentecostal church. We both went to the same Christian school, and I heard his parents praying in tongues. Naturally, I asked, and the answer I received piqued my understanding of the nature of spiritual gifts in modern times for nearly the next two decades. But what does the Bible say? No one ever showed me a biblical explanation explaining when and why the gifts of the Spirit had left the church.

This book is not written to provoke doctrinal arguments in the body of Christ. If you bought this book for that reason, please return it and get your money back. I am not selling proverbial bullets for your religious gun. This book doesn't focus on demons or even name angels. This book was written because being a Christian without having an accurate understanding of the miraculous realm is like driving a car without understanding the road rules. It's like investing in the stock market without understanding the fundamentals of the markets. It's like trying to write a book without knowing your ABCs.

When you are truly "born again," something takes place in the miraculous realm. You are a spiritual creature that lives in a body with a soul. If you never grasp the fundamentals of the miraculous realm, you can miss all the wonderful and intimate things that Jesus Christ intended for you to experience on earth through the person of the Holy Spirit.

John 16:7 says, "It is expedient for you that I go away: for if I go not away, the Comforter will not come unto you; but if I depart, I will send him unto you."

The word "expedient" in Greek means "to be better for, be an advantage, be good and profitable." What was it that Jesus told His disciples would be better for them if He left and the Comforter came? What was the driving force that caused Jesus Christ to die willingly on the cross? What were the mysteries for which all the apostles fought and died that the church could learn about? Why did they write dozens of exciting pass-around letters to the other believers in other regions of the world? And what was it the new believers were supposed to learn?

Memoirs of the Miraculous was written to answer some of the biblical questions many people continue to ask about the miraculous realm as I asked as a child. I pray this book dispels any unbiblical, preconceived notion you may have. I hope the power of the Holy Spirit of Jesus Christ will ignite a fresh passion in you, and especially in your relationship with Him, by a deeper understanding of the miraculous realm.

Early Experiences

"Son, you have to understand. That stuff isn't for today's church. We don't need that now," the man said.

"Where does the Bible say that?" I asked.

"Well, 1 Corinthians 13:9-10 says, 'For we know in part, and we prophesy in part. But when that which is perfect is come then that which is in part will be done away.' When Jesus came, we didn't need that gift anymore, and when the Holy Spirit inspired the Bible through the original twelve apostles, that perfected things. We don't need the Holy Spirit working like that because we have the Bible."

What is the problem with this doctrine? Where is the danger in this? Isn't the Word of God enough? The problem is that no one should ever take one scripture out of the Bible and base an entire doctrine on that scripture. The problem is that from the front of the Bible to the very end, the Holy Spirit is working in and through His people to confirm the scripture. The Scripture is given to us as divine instructions to follow and examples to use as a blueprint from which we build our Christian experiences. Nowhere in the Scripture does it ever say that the power of the Holy Spirit quits working through His people. Nowhere in Scripture does it ever say the gifts of the Holy Spirit worked only through the first twelve apostles. As a matter of fact, the Scripture teaches quite the opposite. All through the Scripture, it clarifies the New Testament church being established through gifts working through men. The Bible without the Spirit giving it life produces mere religion!

Even if you do believe this doctrine we are talking about, called Secessionism, you may also believe we are living in the last days; Jesus Christ is about to return for His church and is preparing the body of Christ for the second coming and the greatest revival the world has ever known. The Scripture says, in the last days, He will pour out His Spirit on "all" flesh. In Greek, in context, the Scripture describes everyone who is willing, the remnant! If you believe this is the time of the last days before Jesus returns, then the Spirit will release prophesy, dreams, visions, signs, and wonders. All these things don't contradict the Scripture; they confirm it.

What's the danger of believing this type of doctrine that was birthed by one man in a college lecture in South Carolina in the late 1800s because he never was filled with the Holy Spirit? Many go on not to believe in the miraculous realm at all!

First Corinthians 12:1-11:

> Now concerning spiritual gifts, brethren,
> I would not have you ignorant. Ye know
> that ye were Gentiles, carried away unto
> these dumb idols, even as ye were led.

Wherefore I give you to understand, that no man speaking by the Spirit of God calleth Jesus accursed: and that no man can say that Jesus is the Lord, but by the Holy Ghost. Now there are diversities of gifts, but the same Spirit. And there are differences of administrations, but the same Lord. And there are diversities of operations, but it is the same God which worketh all in all. But the manifestation of the Spirit is given to every man to profit withal. For to one is given by the Spirit the word of wisdom; to another the word of knowledge by the same Spirit; To another faith by the same Spirit; to another the gifts of healing by the same Spirit; To another the working of miracles; to another prophecy; to another discerning of spirits; to another divers kinds of tongues; to another the interpretation of tongues: But all these worketh that one and the selfsame Spirit, dividing to every man severally as he will.

The Vow

It was a night I'll never forget! An empty beach with the waves crashing down on the East Coast shore; the moon was the only light, however, unusually bright this night. It seemed as if I walked for miles without seeing a soul though I was looking carefully. I had just left the Pier, a bar on Jax Beach in Jacksonville, Florida. It was my eighteenth birthday. I was alone, on the "streets," drunk, and miles away from what I used to call home. I was angry, scared, hurt, confused, depressed, and deceived, all at once.

It was unusually cold for an August summer night, but then again, so was my heart. "God, why have You let this happen to me? Why have You done this to my life? If You are so powerful, why can't You do anything for me? If this is Jesus, I don't want You! Can You hear me, God? Are You listening to me?" No thunder, no fireworks, no help, and no God. "That's what I thought, nothing! There is no real spirit realm. There's no real God, nor devil!"

The clouds seemed to move across the sky, quickly darkening the light that I once had, and then darkness filled my head. Then again, darkness had been filling my head for years, slowly and subtly without notice, gradually bringing me to this place where I now stood. "Satan, if you are real, I call upon you. Nothing?"

I've often asked myself that question. What was it that caused my perception of life and my view of God to become so twisted, especially about the spirit realm, that I would "sell" my soul to Satan? Was it the compromises I had made with my choices of music or movies? Was it that one sip that turned into just one more drink, or that one hit that turned into just one more lie? Did I barter my soul away in a thousand little compromises long before I actually "sold" it?

Where did this mess start? Who or what did it start with? Was it the people I chose to be around, the places I chose to go or was it the latest trend I chose to follow? All these questions have surfaced as I looked back on that night on August 16th, 1991.

I grew up in a Christian home and spent most of my school years in a Christian school. I heard someone preaching the Bible every day of my life. The memorization of scripture was part of my academic curriculum. The problem wasn't a lack of hearing the Word; the problem was actually taking that knowledge and activating it into me by the spirit of Christ.

You see, I knew about Jesus, but I didn't have a personal relationship with Him. At age seven, I went down to the altar, said a prayer of salvation, and joined the church. Nothing was wrong with the prayer of salvation I prayed. The problem was my understanding of salvation. I thought if I said this magic prayer, it was my ticket into heaven. I thought I could come to church, clock in and clock out, leave and continue to live in sin, with no change. Christianity is not that superficial; it's a lifestyle!

At age thirteen, I felt the call into ministry on my life, but there was a problem. My foundation was based on religion and not a relationship with Jesus. When life's trials and temptations came, my foundation crumbled! I started making poor choices about where I would go and what I would do. By age fourteen, I was tripping (getting high on LSD). By age seventeen, my parents divorced; I was a drug addict, and I was living on the streets.

This dysfunctional lifestyle brought me to that point on my eighteenth birthday on a beach in Jacksonville, Florida. Soon after that night, I became ambitious about selling drugs. I moved in with a group that was involved in Wicca, a form of Paganism. I sold drugs to all types of people in all types of places. Some people were heavily involved in witchcraft, such as Satanism and Santeria. Some were involved in the Mexican and Dixie mafia. Others were involved in Hell's Angels, and I also had contact with lots of well-known band groups, such as 311 and Widespread Panic.

During these years, I grew really close to a preacher in the church of Satan. The reverend and a high priest in Santeria mentored me. Throughout this time, I saw crazy things. One day in particular, I saw a guy in the Dixie mafia who was involved in "witchcraft" release a lightning-like power source from his fingertips. My friends involved in Santeria and Satanism would actually "bless" nightclubs and businesses in the Atlanta area with spells and incantations. I actually saw two of my roommates who were involved in a satanic band become possessed by demons, speak to each other in a demonic unknown tongue, and then question me about my views on sin. While living with Satanists in a warehouse, the demonic oppression was so strong that while under the influence of cocaine, I actually drank my own blood, and I did so without knowing why I was doing it.

After five years of this lifestyle, my brother asked me to help him establish a bar and grill in South Carolina. I wasn't exactly thrilled about leaving the fast-paced lifestyle of Atlanta, but I knew I needed change. Before I left, the Santeria priest released many incantations through spells, stones, herbs, and tarot cards over me, my brother, and the business we were about to establish. For the next two years of my life, the bar and grill prospered, and so did the drug business. With this success I had longed for as a teenager came a very heavy price to pay. I had become a paranoid, greedy, and miserable drug addict. Snorting, shooting cocaine, and eating as many hits of ecstasy or acid as I could without overdosing, I started to flirt with suicide.

The more destructive my behavior became, the greater

my desire to become a part of this occult network. I realized that my ties to these people stemmed from that night on the beach in Jacksonville, Florida. During this time, a demon spirit started revealing himself to me. It began tempting me with ideas about ruling the underworld and the business world through its demonic power.

Over the years, I have met thousands of people that seemed to have been blinded by the same darkness that blinded me and has come to saturate America's culture. Whether from movements, fads, or trends, somehow, a whole generation of teenagers has had their minds desensitized and darkened from the light of Jesus Christ, just as I did.

Over the seven years of my occult experiences, I learned about the miraculous realm from a perverted, twisted, and unbiblical foundation. Yet, there was one thing that I was always reminded of. The miraculous realm was real, despite what I had formerly believed. All through my experimenting with the demonic spiritual realm, in the back of my mind was a thought, *What if the Holy Spirit was real and did really work today! If I am experiencing this power now, now would that be like?*

Introduction to the Holy Spirit's Realm

Have you ever had a moment in your life when you stopped, looked around, and thought, *How did I get here?* On August 16, 1998, I looked around and found myself surrounded by leaders from the church of Satan and from the Santeria occult. I was about to be inducted into the army of Satan. For the first time in my life, I suddenly could see what I was becoming, and it scared me to death! Or should I say it scared me to life!

On my twenty-fifth birthday, seven years to the day after that night on the beach, I drove to Atlanta to surprise my friends and celebrate my birthday. I was the one in for the biggest surprise on this night. When I got to the club, one of the most popular rave bars in Atlanta at that time, all my friends in this network were waiting for me. I told no one that I was traveling there that night. Friends from all over the country just happened to be there.

Toward the end of the night, my mentor, the Satanic high priest, walked me into the DJ booth to show me something. He pointed over a sea of people dancing and asked me to look at their new "artwork." As I looked over the crowd, I saw a painting of a dark angel with its wings spread, and in the corner, I saw a dark outline of Jesus. Nobody else could see the paintings unless they were in the DJ booth. The dark reverend turned around, looked me in the eyes, and with his hands wide open, made an offer to be a partner in his business and a "brother" in his network.

At the very moment he turned around with his arms wide open and looked me in the eyes, a voice spoke to me and said, "Heaven is real, hell is real, and you have to make a choice." I became completely conscious of my spiritual state and could sense an overshadowing of the Holy Spirit. The drugs and alcohol seemed to fade away, and conviction from the Holy Spirit was the only thing on my mind. I spent the rest of the night listening to my mentor tell me his master plan of how we were going to become millionaires within a year, but all I could think about was getting back to South Carolina and finding that old dusty Bible that I had packed away years ago.

On August 16, 1998, I made a choice to serve God no matter what, and I was filled with the Holy Spirit. I started to experience the gifts of the Spirit in my life. I went to the Lord in prayer and told Him I would serve Him however He wanted me to, but I had problems. I wanted to be completely free from all satanic bondage. I immediately started reading the Bible, day and night. Every time the desire to do drugs, to commit a sexual sin, or to succumb to temptation came, I pulled out that old Bible and started reading the Word out loud. No matter what temptation or trial came my way, the Word of God brought me victory. Every hex, every vex, and every spell on my life was broken by faith in the power of God's Word and the manifestation of the gifts of the Spirit.

I was so determined to be free that I took the Bible with me into my own bar and grill. I read it between serving beers to customers. My friends would come up and cut lines of cocaine on the bar, tempting me, but the power of God's Holy Word kept me steadfast. I received my complete deliverance from drugs, alcohol, and all satanic bondage through the Word with absolutely no DTs or side effects. And I have kept my deliverance through the Word.

After leaving Atlanta that night, I never tried to call or contact any of those friends again. I began to fast and pray for their salvation. Over the next six months, I experienced extreme demonic oppression. Demons started to manifest themselves in my home, telling me they were going to kill me. They were trying to scare me. People would astro-project into my home, trying to influence my mind through witchcraft and spy on what I was doing. (Astro-projecting is a spiritual action when people, through witchcraft, travel out of their bodies in a spirit form.) Through prayer, fasting, the gifts of the Spirit, and the Word of God, I received complete victory from all spiritual warfare.

One year later, I found out the nightclub they owned

had completely shut down. Every person involved in that network had disappeared from the area. The high priest of the Santeria cult threw himself in front of an Atlanta MARTA transit bus; however, he did not die. When I prayed for these people, I wanted to see them changed by God; I did not want to see them dead. One new Christian, filled with God's Spirit and quoting God's Word, can shut down a whole occultist network!

I found there was a real spirit realm and the Holy Spirit was totally supreme in this realm. He wants you operating in fullness in this realm and wants you to experience all the benefits of the gifts of the Holy Spirit in your life, now!

The Miraculous Realm through Scripture

First Corinthians 12:7-11 says:

> But the manifestation of the Spirit is given to every man to profit withal. For to one is given by the Spirit the word of wisdom; to another the word of knowledge by the same Spirit; to another faith by the same Spirit; to another the gifts of healing by the same Spirit; to another the working of miracles; to another prophecy; to another discernment of spirits; to another divers tongues; to another interpretation of tongues: But all these worketh that the one and the selfsame Spirit, dividing to every man severally, as he will.

The first few months after my salvation experience, I was not in church, and I didn't know a great deal about the Scriptures. I was very vulnerable when it came to the spirit realm. I did not understand who I was in Jesus Christ. And every demon on assignment took full advantage of my lack of knowledge. In the miraculous realm, I stuck out like a sore thumb.

During this time, I had been reading my Bible, but I was having a hard time understanding and remembering the Scriptures. I knew that I had stayed completely free from drug addiction and other sins I was previously in bondage to before I got saved, and I knew my freedom was because of the Word of God.

Before I was saved, these sins had overpowered me and entangled my life. I was not aware of the bondage until after I was saved. After I was saved and filled with the Holy Spirit, I stopped acting on all the previous sins and was ten times more sensitive to the temptations of the sins because of the "gift of discernment of spirits." My mind was being purified by the water of the washing of the Word, and sin stuck out like blood in snow. I thought I was going crazy because of the mental attacks on my mind. Demonic manifestations became almost a common occurrence in my apartment. Nighttime was the worst. I would be tormented by thoughts of fear, and finally, after I would fall asleep, I would have nightmares all night only to wake up to my bed levitating an inch or two off the ground.

Overcoming Fear

Sometimes, I saw physical manifestations of demons, but one thing was for sure: I was a new person and free from the bondage of sin. Every time I called the name of Jesus, all the demonic attacks ceased for a while, and the demons would leave reluctantly.

I knew my situation was serious, and I needed a breakthrough in my life. Being alone and ignorant of the spirit world, I needed help! After three months of this spiritual stalemate, one morning, two demonic beings manifested at the foot of my bed. I looked up to see two semi-transparent silhouettes so tall their heads nearly touched the ceiling. They looked like something from the Arnold Schwarzenegger movie *Predator*. I could see them vaguely but still see through them. My bedroom was filled with an atmosphere of terror. As I looked in horror, one of them said, "We are going to kill you."

At this point, I was sick and tired of living in fear, and I began to notice that, although I was more aware of these attacks, they couldn't control or hurt me. They had been able to use fear only to scare me. I had also noticed that before I was saved, they weren't as visible, and they had more control over my life. After I received Christ as my Savior, they kept their distance from me and used tactics of fear and intimidation. I knew there was a reason they wouldn't come near me.

Satan's kingdom is the opposite of God's kingdom. Satan has no creative power. He can only pervert what God has created. Satan himself was created by God. God's kingdom operates on faith, while Satan's operates on fear. Fear is a dominant factor in Satan's kingdom. Satan will try to use fear in spiritual warfare, and usually, it is his first tactic.

In 2 Timothy 1:7, God says, "For God hath not given us the spirit of fear; but of power, and of love, and of a sound mind." As children of God, we can be completely free from fear because we are children of the Most High God. The psalms tell us we can serve God without fear. Once you begin to understand your authority as a believer, you will become completely free from fear. When you do, watch out! You will start to see major victories in your life as a believer.

At the point these two beings threatened to kill me, a holy boldness rose up from within me. I rose from my bed, and with authority, yelled at the top of my lungs, "If you kill me, I'm going to heaven, and you are not. So leave in the name of Jesus!" Immediately both creatures disappeared. Then, the room filled with the peace of God. From that point on, the demonic manifestations began to stop, and I began to see how powerful God really was in the miraculous realm.

I began to praise God daily, talk to Him like two friends

would talk, and read the Word from the time I would get home until I would fall asleep. Many nights I would fall asleep reading the Bible and wake up the next morning on top of the Word. One night, as I was talking to God in my bedroom, I felt something on the top of my head. It felt as if something was being torn from the center of my brain. It hurt, but for some reason, I knew it came from God. I couldn't explain it, but I had the peace of God. For the next five to ten minutes, this feeling in my head continued. All of a sudden, in the very same place that I felt the tearing, an electric, euphoric feeling filled every single molecule of me. I could only cry and praise God! It felt like electric glory! The Bible describes this feeling as "rivers of living water."

As the weeks went by, the more I prayed, fasted, and read the Word, the deeper this glory went into my body. Eventually, the glory consumed my whole body. As I began to ask God what was happening to me, He told me He had taken me personally through what was known as "deliverance." This phenomenon is commonly referred to as exorcism.

During this time, I was still managing the bar and grill, so the transition from work to home was always tough spiritual warfare. I often read the Bible in the bar while serving alcohol to customers. I never preached to them or anything like that, but I knew if I was going to truly stay free from sin in this environment, I would have to go to the extreme. Every time a demonic manifestation started, I quoted one of the two scriptures I had memorized, and they stopped.

By my sixth month of being saved, God supernaturally led me to a church that preached the uncompromised Word of God. People could worship God without any restraint. The atmosphere there was liberating. It encouraged me to know I wasn't the only Christian who had a relationship with God. As these months went by, I started to see greater victory in spiritual warfare than ever before. God poured out His Spirit anywhere and answered all types of prayers from the biggest to the smallest.

On one occasion, I could see demonic manifestations but no angelic manifestations. The Lord told me that His holy angels were humble and did not want to take any glory away from Him, but the demons were very prideful and wanted me to focus on them so they could receive perverted honor and glory. He said my focus should not be on demons but on Him and His Word. He also said that if they tried to manifest, I should take authority over them in the name of Jesus, and they would leave.

My relationship with Christ started to become like that shared by best friends. I stopped managing the bar and grill and started fellowshipping with other believers. Spiritually, I had ultimate peace. There were still demonic attacks and manifestations, but they were not as frequent and did not last as long.

House Cleaning in the Miraculous Realm

The Holy Spirit prompted me to clean my house from all occult objects. This was a process. Through teaching from my church and my own personal experiences, I learned that the reason these demonic manifestations were happening was that there were "open doors" in my apartment. I prayed over my house many times and did some spiritual house cleaning.

Ephesians 4:27 says, "Neither give place to the devil." The scripture actually should have been translated, "Neither give the devil a place to stand." You see, Satan has to have a legal right to operate. Whether it is unrepented sin in your life or an occult object in your presence, he has to have a right to operate.

One night, during a full moon, I was moving furniture around in my apartment in preparation for a move into a new house. As I was moving a bedroom dresser, I found a black leather lipstick case with a crystal in it. Two years before, I had had a relationship with a girl whom I had gotten pregnant. She had an abortion. During the abortion, her best friend, who was a Wiccan witch, cast a spell in order to catch the spirit of the unborn baby and put it in the crystal.

After the abortion, she gave the crystal to me in a black leather lipstick case and told me what she had done. So two years later, I found this crystal under the bedroom dresser. I am a new creature in Christ now. I did not understand that once a baby dies, its spirit goes back to God. I picked up the black leather case and opened it. I took out the crystal and held it firmly in my right hand as I remembered my unborn child and the circumstances. As I began to meditate on the whole situation, an evil presence started to manifest in the hand that I was holding the crystal. I could feel it start to go up my arm and spread to the rest of my body. I immediately dropped the crystal on the floor and rebuked the spirit in the name of Jesus over and over again.

I then called a friend from the church I was attending and told him what had just happened to me. He told me to hold on and he would call someone from the church leadership to counsel me. When the leadership called, God had already told this person the name of this demonic spirit. Through a word of knowledge, the name that the Lord identified was "Moloch," the god of child sacrifice in the Old Testament. I repented of my part in the situation, took authority over Moloch, cast it out of my apartment, and got rid of the black case and the crystal. Once I did these things, the peace and presence of God were quickly ushered back into my apartment.

Spiritual house cleaning is an ongoing process. There are many different instances where other people "open doors" through the television or the internet. As in times past, I had to pray and ask God why these demonic forces were able to be in my house. God would then show me their "legal right" of entrance.

Deuteronomy 7:25-26 says:

> The graven images of their gods shall ye burn with fire: thou shalt not desire the silver or gold that is on them, nor take it unto thee, lest thou be snared therein: for it is an abomination to the Lord thy God, neither shalt thou bring an abomination into thine house, lest thou be a cursed thing like it: but thou shalt utterly detest it, and thou shalt utterly abhor it; for it is a cursed thing.

God clearly warns us in His Word to keep our houses clean from all occult objects. Talismans, music, movies, or anything else that could be tied to the occult are harmful. If you fail to believe and obey, a curse will come upon your home, your family, and your life.

During this first year of my Christian life, I faced many battlefield lessons I experienced that you can avoid. Avoiding isolation from Christians, reading and quoting God's Word, overcoming fear, and keeping your home as well as body (God's temple) clean are excellent starts to living a lasting victorious Christian lifestyle that God intended for you to live.

God has given you His Word and empowered you with the precious Holy Spirit. He will keep you and guide you into all truth. "Trust in the Lord with all your heart; and lean not unto thine own understanding. In all thy ways acknowledge him, and he shall direct thy paths" (Proverbs 3:5-6).

Slain in the Spirit

"Is this real, God? That guy has to be pushing them down! They can't be just falling out like that. He is knocking them down! If I go up there for prayer, you are going to have to knock me down yourself, God!" Those were my words with God during a revival I attended the first year I was saved. A minister had come from South Africa to preach a week's revival. He preached a little and then called someone out of the crowd. He prayed over them, and bam! They fell down to the ground. Sometimes they shook as if they were hooked up to a high-powered outlet and were getting electrocuted. He was preaching a tremendous message, but I just couldn't make it past the dramatic display at the altar. He was praying in the name of Jesus Christ, but I had never seen anything like this demonstration. I wasn't really sure if the movements going on were even in the Bible.

> Jesus therefore, knowing all things that should come upon him, went forth, and said unto them, Whom seek ye? They answered him, Jesus of Nazareth. Jesus saith unto them, I am he. And Judas also, which betrayed him, stood with them. As soon then as he had said unto them, I am he, they went backward, and fell to the ground.

John 18:4-6

The word "fall" (pip'-to, pet'-o) in this scripture means "to fall (literally or figuratively), fail, fall (down), light on." It doesn't mean that the person has to be knocked out unconscious or unaware. It doesn't mean that the person has to lose memory or will. It gives us a clear picture that whenever the glory of God comes around man, our flesh will fail and fall in some capacity.

As I started to read the Scripture, I saw many times in the Bible words describing the manifestation of the Spirit in a miraculous realm where people simply "fell out."

Daniel 8:15-18:

> And it came to pass, when I, even I Daniel, had seen the vision, and sought for the meaning, then, behold, there stood before me as the appearance of a man. And I heard a man's voice between the banks of Ulai, which called, and said, Gabriel, make this man to understand the vision. So he came near where I stood: and when he came, I was afraid, and fell upon my face: but he said unto me, Understand, O son of man: for at the time of the end shall be the vision. Now as he was speaking with me, I was in a deep sleep on my face toward the ground: but he touched me, and set me upright.

The word "sleep" (raw-dam) in this scripture literally means "to stun, that is, stupefy (with sleep or death), (be fast asleep, be in a deep, cast into a dead, that) sleep (-er, -eth)."

It gives the impression that when the door was open in the miraculous realm, Daniel was zapped as if he were shocked with a stun gun but without the negative side effects. The main reason here for this visitation was to empower and guide Daniel for his destiny, but despite the main purpose, his flesh still had a strange reaction when the door to the spirit realm was open.

"Well, this is the Old Testament, Brother Shawn Patrick. That was yesterday and only happened to the Old Testament prophets and the first twelve apostles of the Lamb. This doesn't happen today for everyone else."

Oh, really? I know another story of a guy who was around after the crucifixion and resurrection but seemed to have the same experience in the miraculous realm. His name was Saul.

> And Saul, yet breathing out threatening and slaughter against the disciples of the Lord, went unto the high priest, And desired of him letters to Damascus to the synagogues, that if he found any of this way, whether they were men or women, he might bring them bound

unto Jerusalem. And as he journeyed, he came near Damascus: and suddenly there shined round about him a light from heaven: And he fell to the earth, and heard a voice saying unto him, Saul, Saul, why persecutest thou me?

Acts 9:1-4

The Greek word for "fell" here in Acts 9:4 is pip'-to, pet'-o, which is the same as in John 18:6, but in this context, it's after the crucifixion and resurrection. Here is another example of this manifestation of the miraculous realm happening, and never can we find a reference in the scripture that it stopped, was an emotional experience, or was a demon.

"God, if You are going knock me out at the altar, do it for real. I want to know that it's really You!" That was my prayer the last night of the revival that the South African minister preached. I had read in the Bible where it happened, but could it happen to me?

As the man started to give the altar call this last night, he looked dead at me and said, "Oh, man, God said He is going to show You that it's Him."

He asked me to come up to the front, and I did. I started walking up to have this man pray for me when all of a sudden, bam! I fell backward at the altar, shaking under the power of the Holy Spirit without anyone laying a finger on me. I lay there for a while in complete peace. I was fully aware I was on the carpet and could hear things around me. I started to get up after a few minutes, but every time I tried, the power of God knocked me back down. I tried three times, and by this time, the entire church was laughing at my fighting with God on the matter. Finally, I lay there without trying to move, and I heard a still small voice speak to my heart, "Stop fighting me. I want to tell you something."

Foreknowledge

I was in between two realms, the natural and the miraculous realm. It was about 7 a.m., and my eyes were closed, but my spirit and mind were wide open. I had been attending an anointed church meeting every night that week and was praying late every night. As I lay there preparing to get up and get my day going, the still small voice of the Holy Spirit spoke something so clear to me that my life has never been the same.

He whispered, "Foreknowledge is sure knowledge!"

God's Word says, "But the manifestation of the Spirit is given to every man to profit withal. For to one is given by the Spirit the word of wisdom; to another the word of knowledge by the same Spirit" (1 Corinthians 12:7-8).

The word "knowledge" (gno'-sis) here means "knowing (the act); that is (by implication) knowledge: knowledge, sense."

Could you ever just sense something about a situation or a person? Maybe in your prayer time or when you got around a certain person or place? You might call it a "gut feeling" or "leading," but however you want to phrase it, the Scripture calls that spiritual function a "word of wisdom" and/or a "word of knowledge."

You must understand that you were created as a spiritual creature, with a soul in a body. Your spirit, when reborn by the spirit of Jesus Christ, will function in certain ways. The more your three-part being "taps" into the miraculous realm, the more frequently a believer might experience functions of the miraculous realm like those mentioned in this chapter.

Even while writing this chapter, I flew to the Gathering Church in Sherman, Texas. We had three services planned; two at one of the local colleges. During a time of prayer before one of the services, the Holy Spirit led me to really deal with the truth that my past was not my future. I could not let this idea go. That night I talked about forgiveness and releasing past hurts to God so that He could change our individual stories—exactly what God does! I just had an overwhelming feeling that someone in the service was dealing with past hurts and, until that person handed them over to God, he or she would allow the past hurts to limit any advancement into the life God had planned.

At the end of the message, we had a wonderful altar time. Many people came forward to receive Christ. As I was praying over people, I stood before a middle-aged couple. I simply sensed that their past had been volatile, and they had survived something tragic. I told them if they would forgive others and let go of the past, God would change their future from hurt to healing and even use their story to help many people. Then I moved to pray for others who came forward.

After the service, the man came to me and asked if I knew who they were or anything about them.

I said, "No, I don't even know your name."

He began to tell me that fourteen years earlier, his daughter and two grandchildren had been brutally murdered. The story had been on national news. He and his wife had never recovered from the tragedy. They came to the meeting asking God to help them move on, and that is exactly what God did! This kind of working of the Spirit might seem strange, but it changes people's lives forever.

Experiences like this one have happened to me hundreds of times, to the point that I simply can't ignore God's workings in the miraculous realm.

John 16:13-15 confirms the truth of the Holy Spirit's supernatural work:

> Howbeit when he, the Spirit of truth, is come, he will guide you into all truth: for he shall not speak of himself; but whatsoever he shall hear, that shall he speak: and he will shew you things to come. He shall glorify me: for he shall receive of mine, and shall shew it unto you. All things that the Father hath are mine: therefore said I, that he shall take

of mine, and shall shew it unto you.

The word "guide" (hod-ayg-eh'-o) in this scripture means "to show the way (literally or figuratively [teach]), guide, lead." The Holy Spirit is on assignment in your life to lead and guide you in your purpose in Christ and to help you lead others in their purpose. This assignment is one of the reasons why He has come.

You may think, *Well, yes, of course, God does convict us of our sins and testifies of Jesus Christ, but stop right there, Shawn Patrick, and wait a second. Jesus was speaking to the first twelve apostles, not to us believers today.* Let's keep the context of this scripture and look on down a little bit and see just exactly who Jesus was referring to in this context.

In John 17:20-23, we find these words of Jesus:

> Neither pray I for these alone, but for them also which shall believe on me through their word; That they all may be one; as thou, Father, art in me, and I in thee, that they also may be one in us: that the world may believe that thou hast sent me. And the glory which thou gavest me I have given them; that they may be one, even as we are one: I in them, and thou in me, that they may be made perfect in one; and that the world may know that

thou hast sent me, and hast loved them,
as thou hast loved me.

That's me and you, my friend! The Holy Spirit wants to establish His kingdom in you and through you. If you learn to recognize His leadings and obey His still small voice, you will see the spirit of the Lord do incredible things in your life. The more you obey, the more you see the miraculous realm open up in your everyday life!

What Did He Say?

"It's Bible study time. If you are coming, come on! You only have an hour left," I yelled on the PE field as about twenty youth came running up to the outdoor buildings in the back of the school. I was a counselor at a troubled-teen facility for ten years. For ten years, I held Bible studies fifteen days a month. We had over a thousand youth saved out there during this period. An interesting thing is that these Bible studies were in a private room, where I learned to flow with the spirit of God in a service. The teenagers there came hungry for the presence of God like you wouldn't believe. I always led worship for thirty minutes or so, preached a message, and laid hands on whoever wanted prayer. This teen facility is the place where I learned to hear the spirit of God ministering to people.

During one particular service, we had a few gang members from LA, suburban kids from Charlotte, NC, and a nice blend of diversity of other backgrounds. Many had never been in church; some were raised Catholic, some Mormon, some Baptist, and some agnostic. As I opened the service, I was praising God as I sang, "I went to the enemy's camp." We sang and praised until these guys were sweating up a storm. We could all sense the presence of God so strongly that every voice in the room fell into total silence. The tangible person of the Holy Spirit was so real that teens were weeping like small children. All of a sudden, a young man raised Catholic burst out, speaking in an unknown tongue. He looked as if he was extremely surprised, and many of the young men did as well. A moment of silence went by.

"Mr. Shawn. This is crazy, but I think I heard in English what he just said in whatever langue he just said it," said a young African American that never grew up in church and was a Folk Nation gang member from LA. He said he heard a message about these youth growing up to be ministers in America after God called them to repentance. As he gave the message, these kids started crying out to Jesus Christ with a passion I had rarely heard.

"But the manifestation of the Spirit is given to every man to profit withal…to another divers kinds of tongues; to another the interpretation of tongues" (1 Corinthians 12:7,10).

After I had been saved and had attended church for a year or so, I went to my pastor about an issue. He had asked one of the church's elders to attend the meeting because he knew I had come from the occult and a major drug addiction. During the counseling session, he asked me if I had my prayer language. I didn't have a clue what he was talking about.

He said, "Praying in the Holy Ghost."

What Did He Say?

I said, "I want everything God has for me. I want whatever gift He gives if I can have it."

He laid hands on me. I prayed to receive the gift of the Holy Spirit and all He had for me. I opened my mouth, and my lips began speaking. I was watching my lips move, but I wasn't the one moving them. I initially started opening my mouth, but God took over. I couldn't understand a word that was coming out of my mouth. I fell out on the floor, still speaking in an unknown tongue. I felt the power of God all over me as if I had been plugged into an electrical massage. I got up off the ground and felt a thousand pounds lighter. I had a spiritual and biblical experience that totally changed my life.

I have been in services where I observed people speaking in tongues and someone else gave an interpretation. I sometimes have given the interpretation. There have been times when no one gives an interpretation, and the person sits down as the service moves on. I also have seen someone speak in tongues and someone in the service tell what they said in a different country's language. I pray in tongues every day. Sometimes I pray in tongues before and during my preaching meetings. The bottom line is that I observe many different types of manifestations of speaking in tongues, of which all are completely scriptural. The Holy Spirit will use this gift in many ways to empower, edify, and bless His people.

First Corinthians 14:2, 4, 13, and 14:

> For he that speaketh in an unknown tongue speaketh not unto men, but unto God: for no man understandeth him; howbeit in the spirit he speaketh mysteries... He that speaketh in an unknown tongue edifieth himself; but he that prophesieth edifieth the church... Wherefore let him that speaketh in an unknown tongue pray that he may interpret. For if I pray in an unknown tongue, my spirit prayeth, but my understanding is unfruitful.

In closing this chapter, I want to say that many people and many churches have been divided on the topic of speaking in tongues. The people that do not understand the gift attack those who do it and disassociate with them and any type of function in the body they have. The people who practice it come against those people who don't with anger out of hurt and rejection. They won't associate with those people in the body who don't speak in tongues and look down on them out of spiritual pride. Thus the body of Christ gets more deeply divided on a non-essential issue. We must remember our salvation and core foundation do not depend upon the issue of speaking in tongues.

If you are in a church service where the pastor is preaching

What Did He Say?

or worship is taking place, and the spirit of the Lord is upon you in the manifestation of speaking in tongues, please be mindful of a few things. One, if no interpretation comes through someone else, do not keep on speaking. You will become a distraction to the service rather than the edification of the body. A Sunday morning service at a traditional church has new believers that have no clue what is going on.

I conduct prayer gatherings all over the world, and I know in these settings, at times, prayer warriors will speak in tongues, and maybe a word of interpretation will come, but many times, the prayer warriors are standing in the gap on issues that only the Spirit knows. That setting is fine because most attendees pray in the Spirit and understand what is happening. At a prayer gathering I held in December 2004, we all started weeping, praying in tongues, and travailing in prayer. None really understood what was taking place. This went on for two hours. We all left and knew the Holy Spirit had us standing in the gap for something big. At the same time we were praying, we later found out Indonesia was getting hit with a tsunami that killed hundreds of thousands of people. Praying in tongues allows you to tap into the miraculous realm in a wonderful and mysterious way.

This gift is great and powerful for your spiritual growth if you learn how to incorporate it into your life scripturally and in balance. The devil fights the body of Christ on this gift, especially if this gift is practiced unscriptural and

59

unbalanced. At the time of this writing, the Southern Baptist Convention just changed its policy on its missionaries being able to speak in tongues. This change is a contrast to their former policy, which forbade funding for missionaries who spoke in tongues.

So many missionaries needed this power gift for their front-line work that an estimated fifty percent of them did speak in tongues, even when their denomination forbade it. They now do not forbid the practice and have put out an official statement on it.

Yet, speaking in tongues had become an issue in the past because many people had seen this gift abused or done out of order. Some of them simply just didn't understand how it worked. Never come against something that you don't understand! Fear drives your fight. Stop to consider: What if you are fighting the very hand of God?

Angelic Visitations

Over the years, I have had numerous encounters with the angelic. At the time of this writing, I have had around twenty instances of encounters. I've seen angels stretch by like lighting, balls of light battling with dark balls of energy, translucent forms, and more.

I begin this chapter by sharing one of my most memorable times about angelic experiences. I was in Nigeria, where I spent ten years evangelizing almost every major city in the nation. Many times, I went with a dear friend, a television producer. We had just had a meeting where a lady came in with a soft-ball-sized tumor, and the Lord healed her on the spot.

We were resting in the hotel room that night when all of a sudden, the room was filled with rainbow colors and bright light. I was stunned a bit and then asked my friend if he saw what I was seeing. He then described everything to me in detail. I looked over, and an angel was standing right beside my bed. He had an angel hovering over him singing. It was the most majestic music we had ever heard. This display continued for forty-five minutes. I don't know what I was thinking, but I reached out to touch the leg of the angel to see if I was losing my mind or if it was real. As I reached out to touch the leg, I woke up instantly, and it was morning. I asked my friend if that just really happened, and he woke up at the same time and confirmed the experience. I share this chapter with reservations and questions about real experiences I don't understand, but I share them with hope about what I do understand: We have angels, and they are on our side. Some are fallen angels, and some are not. At times, some of us see them, and at other times on this earth, we can't fully grasp what we've seen. We look to the Bible as our guide and have a strong hope we will see them in heaven.

In 2001, I had been saved for only about a year, and at this point, I experienced a wilderness season. I had cut off most of my friends from my past and had very few new ones from my life after being born again. I spent hours reading my Bible, praying, and worshipping every day. On this particular day, I was praying in my living room, kneeling by the sofa. As I stood up to walk into the kitchen, I saw standing in the bedroom a translucent being. It was about six feet tall and looked to have a robe on. You could see it but also through it at the same time. It zipped through the room and vanished. I could sense the presence of holiness. I started speaking the name of Jesus out loud and started praising God. I had sensed the presence of the Holy Spirit and angels in the past, but this time I caught a glimpse.

Since that time, I have had other encounters with angels. I have seen holy ones and fallen ones. I have never had the same encounter twice, but I write this chapter with holy reverence and holy fear. I want you to understand I am about

Angelic Visitations

to share some stories with you, and I don't fully understand the depth of them, but I do understand the Scriptures give us warnings and positive examples of the many ways angels work on earth in the miraculous realm.

Many cults have been birthed by angels visiting men and giving messages that don't harmonize with Scripture. The bottom line is that angels always give glory to Jesus and stay within the scriptural boundary on their assignments. They are not going to give messages that focus on themselves. That's a perverted form of worship. Any movement or denomination built solely on angelic visitations surely will lead to major error!

"But even if we or an angel from heaven should preach a gospel other than the one we preached to you, let him be eternally condemned!" (Galatians 1:8)

One of the most famous guitar players of all time is Carlos Santana. Santana came to fame back in the seventies, during the time of Woodstock. He actually talks about having a spiritual encounter with a snake that came out of his guitar while he was playing and tripping on LSD. Later in his career, he did interviews on many media outlets about an angelic encounter he had with an angel of light. This angel spoke to him and said this. The entire spiritual experience was based on an angel of light, but it was a fallen angel that was posing as an agent of good.

Snoop Dogg had the spirit of Bob Marley appear to him and say that he was being possessed by the same spirit that was in Marley. Many musical artists practice sorcery and have these "angelic" encounters. The devil and his army have the ability to operate on earth for a time but make no mistake about it; they are part of that one-third of the fallen angels that aren't in hell but on earth. I am not mentioning these artist names to bash on them. That is not my intention. I pray for them. I only point out examples to warn believers. I love people, and God does as well. We are praying for a revival among the entertainment industry and never want to "bash" anyone.

"And no marvel; for Satan himself is transformed into an angel of light" (2 Corinthians 11:14).

The very first time I was led to share my testimony was to witness to someone on a street in Boulder, Colorado. I had never tried but was burning in my belly to be a witness. I really didn't know how or what to say. I didn't understand the Scriptures and wasn't ready but didn't realize it at the time. I saw a guy standing on the corner with really long hair. It was New Year's Eve, and the street was filled with a party atmosphere. This guy looked homeless, and I assumed he was not a believer. I walked up to him and started to make conversation. I noticed his blue, compassionate eyes. I began my spiel, and it was just that, a spiel. Everything I said was wrong and judgmental. I wasn't equipped to hit the battlefield. Instead of leading with God's grace and forgiveness, I was insensitive and assuming. Everything I said, he would counter in a graceful way. I could tell something was different, but I was so caught up in my head to be a "hero" that I missed out on who he was and what he was saying.

By the time I realized how bad I had actually encountered this guy with the gospel and how much more saved this guy seemed to be than I, he was gone. Just like that. I have often wondered if God's grace sent an angel for me to receive a huge lesson in evangelism that would break my flesh about methods of evangelism and shape my ministry's style.

"Be not forgetful to entertain strangers: for thereby some have entertained angels unawares" (Hebrews 13:2).

In 2002, I was married for one year, and my wife and I had felt led by the Spirit to look for another house. We had made a commitment to have children; my wife would stay at home and raise them while I trusted God to provide for the family. The house that we felt the Spirit releasing us to purchase was twice the size and three times the cost of the little start-up home we currently lived in. This new house had a bonus room over the garage, and as soon as I walked in the room, I knew this was to be the Warrior Nations International Ministries headquarters. Our current office was in our bedroom, so this was a big thing for us. The

Holy Spirit told us we would be planning meetings all over the world from this strategic war room. We purchased the house and started moving.

The first week we were in the house, we were totally exhausted from moving. Fear was trying to grip my mind that we could not make the new house payment. My wife and I knew we were in a spiritual battle. We both talked about the mental struggle we were having about not being able to afford the home. We lay down in the bed, and I shut my eyes but was wide awake. The mental battle still raged in my head. Fear-filled thoughts flooded me with fear, doubt, and unbelief. As I lay there struggling in my mind, I saw a white angel and a dark angel fighting above our new home. They both had swords. The white angel had a white sword, and the dark angel had a dark sword. Their swords collided high in the air and then moved swiftly down towards the earth. They went from one end of the property to the other end. This went on for some time. I was wide awake and captivated.

All of a sudden, they were fighting right over my bed. I could have reached out and touched them. Their swords hit right above me, and then they slid down swiftly. Their swords went right into my foot. A sharp pain hit my foot, and I jumped out of the bed and started praying in the Spirit. I was freaked out but knew my prayers were giving the angel strength. The visuals in the miraculous realm faded, but the reality of the miraculous realm didn't. We were in the middle of a spiritual war!

"For we wrestle not against flesh and blood, but against principalities, against powers, against the rulers of the darkness of this world, against spiritual wickedness in heavenly places" (Ephesians 6:12).

Demonic Manifestations

Father's Day 2004 was a church service I will never forget. The Holy Spirit had been dealing with me about how the role of our earthly father can massively distort the view we have of our heavenly Father and how the enemy uses tragic experiences of our childhood to keep us in spiritual bondage as an adult. I had prepared a message teaching on this topic and was preaching the Father's Day service at the small church I first was a pastor. At the end of the service, I gave an altar call for those who had been hurt by their father or unforgiving hearts towards their father.

As the people came forward to respond, I said a very simple prayer. I asked each to ask God first for forgiveness and then forgive their fathers. As each person did this, I simply said that every Satanic power be broken that was working through unforgiveness. "Hissssss" was the next noise I heard. A young lady who came up for prayer said the prayer, but when we broke the power of the spirit attached to that unforgiveness, she started hissing and scratching at me like a cat! She lunged toward me, and I stepped back. The altar worker held her from me, and I took authority over this spirit. After a few minutes, the spirit had left, and she was in her right mind crying and singing praises to the Lord.

In another incident, I was in a community prayer service

interceding for our region and city. We had about four or five churches come together to stand in the gap for revival. We had been worshiping and praying for some time. One of the leaders started to pray against principalities over the city and region. As we began to take authority over the city in Jesus' name, a woman walked in the door. She walked around and acted like she was about to pray. She was acting very strange, but she knew a pastor from a small local fellowship.

"You can't mess with me!" she said in a very demonic tone. I looked at her to see who she was talking to. She started taunting the pastors. She identified herself as one of the principalities we were praying against. She began challenging us. I looked at her and rebuked the spirit in the name of Jesus! She started laughing. I knew it was a showdown. This spirit was trying to bust up a very powerful prayer group.

Loose her in the name of Jesus! I said. She started convulsing, and the pastors stepped in to help me with this deliverance. After twenty minutes, the lady fell out on the ground limp. After talking to her pastor, I found out she practiced a very dangerous error. She had been seeing demonic spirits leave kids and teens in church services and "capturing" them in her body so that they would hurt any of the kids. Over time, this extremely unbiblical practice caused her to become demon-possessed.

"And when He was come to the other side into the country of the Gergesenes, there met him two possessed with devils, coming out of the tombs, exceeding fierce, so that no man might pass that way" (Matthew 8:28).

The one thing you must understand about demonology. First, demons don't want you to think they exist. They want you to believe it is just a movie fiction concept or some made-up fairy tale. If you don't believe they are real, they can't really oppress and possess people without any hindrance. Once they realize you know they're real, they go to plan B. They try to scare you so bad that you run from them. Fear is their weapon against your faith.

"And these signs shall follow them that believe; in my name they shall cast out devils…" (Mark 16:17)

You have all authority over demonic spirits. Don't be afraid and don't allow them to bully you. They will try to manifest and make you fearful, and then they will try to get you to spend all your time fighting them and dealing with them. Jesus is the total authority! Once the spirit world realizes you are not afraid and won't tolerate terrorist-type attacks from them, they will start to leave you alone. They simply try to test if you really believe Jesus is who the Bible says He is in your life!

"Neither give the devil a place to stand" (Ephesians 4:27).

Demons are very territorial and must have a valid reason to oppress a Christian. Many have asked if a Christian can be possessed by a demon. I believe that a blood-bought, spirit-filled Christian will cause a demon to fear. I don't believe that a Christian can be completely possessed, but I do believe that they can be deeply oppressed. Whether a demon is trying to possess or oppress a person, it is still trying to control them. I don't want either one to take place.

The word here in the above scripture for "place" means "room" or "real estate." Don't give the devil a place to work in your life. Christians give the devil place by unconfessed sin, unhealed inner hurts, generational curses, forgiveness, and commissioned territory.

I was saved one year and went to Atlanta with my job. I was with coworkers, and they wanted to go to Five Points downtown. I went with them, and they wanted to go into a store that sold occult supplies. I heard the Holy Spirit say no, but under peer pressure, I went in the store anyway. The lady working in the store saw me and looked at me like she was looking through me at something else. She went to the back of the store. I knew I messed up and left the store. Later that night, I was sleeping and was woke up by a demon that was choking me and lifted me out of my bed. I could not speak. I was paralyzed. Finally, I spoke the name of Jesus, and the spirit left. I repented for my disobedience and broke the hold of that spirit. I went to uncommissioned territory.

"Then goeth he, and taketh with him seven other spirits more wicked than himself, and enter in there and dwell there: and the last state of that man is worse than the first" (Matthew 12:45).

This book is not meant to be a detailed teaching on demonology 101, but you need to know some basics. I have conducted over two hundred or more exorcisms. They come out in Jesus' name! Here is a little advice.

Get biblical counseling as well as deliverance because nine times out of ten, the demon will leave just by your mind receiving the Word of God. You won't even need to go through many times. Most important, if your Word levels are not strong enough and your commitment to following Jesus is not solid, the demons will come back seven times worse.

Discernment of Spirits

I had only been a Christian for a few months and had experienced the Holy Spirit for the first time. One thing I noticed was that the more time I spent in prayer, the more aware I was of His presence. I could sense Him wake me up and manifest while I was in prayer or worship. He would overtake me while I was reading the Bible. It was awesome! But there was something going on that was very disturbing at the same time. I could sense the presence of evil spirits as well.

> For the word of God is quick and powerful, and shaper than any two-edged sword, piercing even to the dividing asunder of soul and spirit, and the joints and morrow, and is a discerner of the thoughts and intents of the heart. Neither is there any creature that is not manifest in His sight...
>
> Hebrews 4:12-13

Am I going crazy? I thought. I didn't get out much in those days. When I would get out of my "bubble" and go in public places, I would have an invasion of demonic thoughts. Sometimes very intrusive images would flash in my head, or I would hear voices when I would get around certain places or people. I began to notice that many times when the thoughts or images I was experiencing came to me, they would be similar to a coinciding situation I would face or someone else would be going through.

I would be having images and thoughts of suicide when I got around people that struggled with it. When I would get around those places or people that were having addiction issues, that would be what intrusively bombarded my mind. If it was pride, fear, etc., that's what I would pick up in the spirit realm. At first, I thought it was just me being tempted, but then I started to realize what the Scripture taught on the matter.

"To another the working of miracles; to another prophecy; to another discerning of spirits…" (1 Corinthians 12:10)

The word "discernment" (dee-ak'-ree-sis) in Greek means "judicial estimation," and the word "spirits" (pnyoo'-mah) in Greek means "a current of air, a breeze, a spirit; that is, the rational soul, mental disposition of an angel, demon, or God, Christ's spirit, the Holy Spirit."

In other words, the gift allows the believer to operate in authoritative evaluation of what type of spirit is working in the mind realm or miraculous realm around them.

Why would you need this? The Holy Spirit gave me an analogy that explains it well. Say you are taking a delightful walk in a field, and all of a sudden, you smell something. It's very sweet and inviting. You keep sniffing, and the aroma is very fresh. You look around to see what you smell, and you see a beautiful row of summer orchards just waiting for you to come over to view their beauty. You walk over to the flowers and enjoy their fragrance.

As you start to walk in the field again, you notice a very different smell. This one stinks! The smell makes you want to gag. It is so bad it overwhelms you with disgust. You stop as soon as you smell it because it smells like cow stinky. You look around, and right before your next step is a pile of cow stinky. You notice it and walk around it. You leave as fast as you can because no one likes stinky.

Your nose and eyes act as warnings to your surroundings when you are around crap. They act as announcements when you are around the sweet aroma of flowers. It is the same way in the miraculous realm. The discernment of spirits allows you to gauge the atmosphere around you and make the necessary adjustment needed to your situation, whether it's to worship or war. I don't think I have to tell you which analogy represents which spirit. You get the picture. This helps you identify the strongman, so you can effectively bind him and spoil his goods.

Don't be quick to presume that just because you are picking up a spirit working in someone's life, they are currently committing the sin that spirit is tempting them to do. This can be very dangerous to the individual you are ministering to if you confront them with an accusation. Pray that not only will you know the origin of the spirit but the operation of it as well.

Before I was saved, I was very sexually active. It was bondage in my life and a secret one. No one really knew how addicted I was, nor what I was doing in my sex life. Most sexual sins are secret ones, and the enemy tries to keep people in long-term sexual bondage by never talking about it. Once I was saved, I made a commitment to be one hundred percent abstained from any sexual activity. I was saving myself for my future wife. I never told anyone about my porn addiction before I was saved, but I never committed it after I was saved.

One night, I went to a meeting to meet a very well-known preacher. He was known for the gifts of the spirit and had been recommended to me by a friend that I met him. I sat through service, and it was Holy Spirit packed. People got saved, and there were many different wonderful things that took place in the service. I waited to talk to the man after service. Everyone left the church, and it was just me, the senior pastor, and this man of God.

He asked me some questions about my conversion and then my call to evangelism. Right in the middle of our conversation, he said to me that I needed to stop committing sexual sin. I looked at him in amazement because it had been well over a year that I had been pure before the Lord in the area of sexual sins. He was very persistent that he was right, and I was lying about it. He was not mean about what he said, but he indicated he didn't believe me.

We know "in part," and that gives us a direction to search out the warning the Holy Spirit is allowing us to pick up, but we will only have a part. Never assume. Be aware of what you are discerning and ask for the spirit of wisdom on the application of it.

Dreams and Visions

And it shall come to pass in the last days,
saith God, I will pour out of my Spirit upon
all flesh: and your sons and daughters
shall prophesy, and your young men shall
see visions and your old men shall dream
dreams.

Acts 2:17

During the first few months I was saved, I read in the Bible that the disciples fasted and prayed during times of need for direction. I was working in a mortgage company and hated it. I had such a burden to preach the gospel but was not going in the direction that I felt I needed to go. I decided to fast and pray all day one Sunday about the issue. It got late, and I went to sleep early, trying to get through my twenty-four-hour fast. I thought I would wake up the next day and eat a huge breakfast. I fell asleep.

I woke up to a strange presence in my room. The hairs all over my body were standing straight up, and I had felt like there was a ghost in my room. I looked over at the clock. "3:33," it said. Just then, I realized I had a dream. In the dream, I was walking through the woods. As I was walking, the forest started to get dark and full of overgrown vines. They were dying, and the deeper I walked into the forest, the darker and more dead the forest became.

I noticed that I started to pass gravestones. One after one, I passed these gravestones. I looked around and found myself surrounded by a graveyard. Right in the middle of the graveyard, there was a card. I walked over to the card and looked at it intently. My name and the name of the mortgage company were on the card. I felt a warning feeling and then woke up.

It didn't take a great deal of inciting to realize God was telling me to get out of the mortgage business. I knew I was called to preach and that business was not a part of my calling. The dream confirmed a conviction. I started looking for a job based on what I felt like God was calling me to do. I enrolled in Bible school and started working with a troubled teen facility at the same time. During my time working there, I started Bible studies, church visits, Christian counseling, deliverance ministry, and much more. We saw over a thousand kids give their life to Jesus during this ten-year period at the school.

Not all dreams are prophetic. Some are a result of what we put in our bodies. Some are a result of what we put in our minds. If you take medication, then you will experience pharmaceutical dreams from time to time. If you watch things on television, you will see those images show up in your dreams many times. Some dreams are demonic and happen when you are under heavy spiritual warfare. Those dreams can have a similar function to the gift of discernment, even though they are not prophetic direction dreams. People with a strong gift of discernment often experience that gift at night through dreams.

Dreams from the Holy Spirit are given for the direction of your destiny. Those dreams act as road signs to your spiritual path. God will use colors, numbers, biblical symbols, and personal past experiences to speak to you about a current situation. He uses natural things and their function to bring a spiritual truth. God isn't trying to trick us by making dreams complicated for us to understand. He wants to speak to us and guide us. Some people receive dreams better than they do prophetic words in prayer.

The more of the Bible that you understand, the deeper your knowledge to understand the dream you have is. One of the most well-known spiritual dream teachers in the body of Christ is John Paul Jackson. I had the privilege of spending the day with him some years ago. He was an awesome man of God, with the love of the Father flowing out of him. He passed away during the writing of this book and was going to write an endorsement for this book. I learned early on that when I have an uncommon time of access with an uncommon man of God, I'm asking questions.

I spent all day with him at the Daystar TV Network

shooting a series on the *Joni* show with him and Joni Lamb. We filmed a five-part series on the miraculous realm. One of the things that he said to me was that he buys a new Bible every year. If he doesn't, he is tempted to go back to the notes of the years past, and that clouds his ability to receive fresh knowledge from God. He is reading through and taking fresh notes on his studies. Over the thirty years of his ministry, he has created a deep Bible understanding that has given him a wonderful ability to understand dreams. John Paul told me that God gave him the gift to understand dreams early on in his Christian walk.

> On the morrow, as they went on their journey, and drew nigh unto the city, Peter went up upon the housetop to pray about the sixth hour. And he became very hungry, and would have eaten: but while they made ready, he fell into a trance, and saw heaven opened...
>
> Acts 10:9-11

On my first time on the JCTV Youth Network, sponsored by the Trinity Broadcasting Network, my publisher and I were driving around the Beverly Hills area looking around. It was my first time in the LA area, and I wanted to check out some of the sights while I was there. I was fascinated with the surroundings and was a true South Carolina tourist.

Dreams and Visions

As we were driving around, I saw something. It was like a flash in my mind. I saw a platform, like a stage, and in the platform, I saw faces. These faces were small so that no one face took up a lot of space on the platform. As I looked again, I saw many familiar faces. Some were Oral Roberts, Kenneth Hagen, Kenneth Copeland, Adrian Rodgers, Amy Simple-McPherson, Williams Seymour, and many others that I didn't recognize. Even the ones that I didn't recognize seemed to have a familiar aura.

There seemed to be a sealant on the floor of the platform. Where the pulpit should be were three warrior spears that shot straight up into the air towards the heavens. I saw this instantly, like a flash, and then back to my normal view of the city. I was very vocal in telling what I saw to my publisher and the team traveling with me.

God called me to a warrior ministry. Our purpose is to raise up an army in this generation for the Lord. Our name and the elements of our ministry reflect that call. God often uses military terms or football symbols when speaking to me. I like and understand football, and the training is similar to military boot camp training, as my high school football coach used.

In the vision, the platform represented all the past moves of the Spirit. The faces were a representation of the men and women of God who started various ministries. The past generations had strong leaders representing each ministry, and their personalities played a big part in the moves. All of them built the platform, but no one person was the focus. The spears were this next generation building upon their work, but they were a nameless and faceless generation. All pointed to the throne. The spears represented the warrior fight inside them. Three of them represented the harmony of the Trinity. I knew this last-day generation would have incredible unity among themselves.

God is using extraordinary measures to reach people all over the world and shift the body of Christ for the last days' outpouring of the Holy Spirit. Dreams and visions form a giant work of the Holy Spirit with His people to guide, confirm, warn, and comfort. Write the dreams and visions down. Don't discredit them as simply coincidence. Look for scriptural meaning and parallel life applications. I promise that if you are diligent in recording your visions and dreams, God will amaze you with His faithfulness in this area.

Prophetic Protocol

We live in a society that has had a four hundred percent increase in occult activities over the past decade, and seventy-three percent of North American college and youth have participated in occult activity in one form or another. There is a hunger for the supernatural realm in America. People are drawn to the miraculous realm, where a thousand ways exist to fulfill that hunger in their inner spirits. People run to physics for a "reading" and look to astrology for starlight guidance. God created us with a curiosity about this realm.

The number one reason most people in the church stay away from studying or practicing the gifts of the Spirit is that they see extremes in certain circles of the body of Christ. As I've preached messages in over twenty-six different denominations, in over twenty-seven different nations all over the world, I've asked pastors tough questions behind the scenes. They have told me "extremism" is the main issue causing them and other leaders to suppress the gifts of the Spirit. I believe they cite a valid point.

The Apostle Paul wrote most of the letters to the New Testament church dealing with order in the church, along with rules on how to judge and address extremism when it took place. Many times, as he saw the confusion that took place amid people who were unaccustomed to the manifestations of the spirit of God, he would require the church leadership to follow guidelines so that those people would not be lost in the excesses of spiritual manifestations. Let's look at some of the biblical guidelines he laid out.

The gift of prophecy is a gift that is biblically supposed to be promoted and celebrated in the body of Christ. I believe in this gift, but we must follow the rules of the Scriptures. According to the Bible, we follow the guidelines in Romans 12:6, "...let us prophesy according to the measure of faith." This gift is applied by faith, and we can grow this gift by using our faith.

It is specific, directive, corrective, and more than general encouragement or comfort. It should be judged by leaders to be confirmed by twos and threes. Paul says, "Let the prophets speak two or three, and let the other judge" (1 Corinthians 14:29).

It should be given in a spirit of love. Even in the Old Testament, the prophets gave God's redemptive plan in the middle of a judgment prophecy. Many people may hear the word of the Lord but give the prophecy in a wrong context and totally misrepresent the heart of God in the matter. Moses was banned from entering the Promised Land for misrepresenting the word of the Lord. Paul says, "And though I have the gift of prophecy, and understand all mysteries, and all knowledge; and though I have all faith, so that I could move mountains, and have not love, I am nothing" (1 Corinthians 13:2). All prophecy is in part. We see through a glass dimly. No one has the whole picture.

We always keep these rules as our guide. Many will presume or misinterpret prophecy and then close it improperly. Many misunderstand what they get, tell someone else, and the result is prophetic gossip, which is not what the Bible teaches. It states clearly, "For we know in part and we prophesy in part" (1 Corinthians 13:9).

Don't despise prophecy because of immature situations that happen. Maybe someone "missed it" when they gave you a word of prophecy. Maybe the prophecy didn't come to pass when or in which way you thought it would. Don't get upset or lose faith in this gift. Above all, don't despise the gift of prophecy. Let's promote it and keep it balanced. Paul says, "Despise not prophesyings" (1 Thessalonians 5:20).

The Bible tells us to long for the Holy Spirit and covet it. Because we promote and believe that the Holy Spirit still speaks, we long for Him to. Paul says, "Wherefore, brethren, covet to prophesy, and forbid not to speak in tongues" (1 Corinthians 14:39).

Prophecy should be open. No "parking lot" prophecies. Watch out for anyone in worship services not following this protocol, so the prophecy may be balanced and correct. Usually, when a secret prophecy occurs, it comes out of immaturity or selfish ambition. A prophetic presbytery needs to be set inside the church to balance and weigh the prophecies. These scriptures in Acts give us examples of this structure. Please read and study the following: Acts 15:2, 4, 6, 22, 23; 16:4; 21:18. Also, Paul says:

> Let the prophets speak two or three, and let the others judge. If anything be revealed to another that sitteth by, let the first hold his peace. For ye all may prophesy one by one, that all may learn, and all may be comforted. And the spirit of the prophets are subject to the prophets.

> 1 Corinthians 14:29-32

The prophetic words you receive over your lifetime will bring hope when your purpose and destiny are challenged by the enemy. Write down what prophecies you get that are confirmed and you know are from God. Those tested words will help you down the road when the test of purpose occurs. Speak back those prophecies to yourself and to the enemy to remind yourself and the devil what God says, not what he says or your situation indicates. As Paul is mentoring young Timothy, he says, "This charge I commit unto thee, son Timothy, according to the prophecies which went before on thee, that thou by them mightest war a good warfare" (1 Timothy 1:18).

Prophetic Protocol

Prophecy should have the fruit of the Spirit to uphold the gift. Pride and manipulation have polluted this gift, keeping it from functioning many times. If prophecy is given without the fruit of the Spirit as its foundation, then "charismatic witchcraft" or "soul force" can happen. When this occurs, it is verified by the Scriptures as false prophets and false prophecies.

This falsification can happen quickly with younger ministers that are trying to get established. Unknowingly, they can operate a strong gift around a hidden agenda or an un-submitted area of their soul. This fallacy demonstrates the importance of following these biblical guidelines. They are so critical in the application of this gift. You can prophesy and cast out devils and still go to hell!

Jesus said, "Beware of false prophets, who come to you in sheep's clothing, but inwardly they are ravenous wolves. Ye shall know them by their fruits" (Matthew 7:15-16).

In the same chapter of Matthew, Jesus said:

Many will say unto me on that day, Lord, Lord, have we not prophesied in thy name? And in thy name cast out devils? And in thy name done many wonderful works? And then I will profess unto them, I never knew you: depart from me ye that work iniquity.

Matthew 7:22-23

If you want to have a healthy prophetic culture at your ministry or in your life, you must allow the foundation to be driven by love. If the atmosphere is loving, then it will be forgiving when people "miss it" as they try to grow in this gift. If the prophecy is not driven by redemption and love, then the prophet needs to sit down until the love capacity is as big as the prophecy capacity. Even in the Old Testament, God gave a redemptive option when the prophet showed up to give a word. How much more should we have redemption in our prophetic culture under the grace of the New Testament!

Miracles Are for Today

Abuja, Nigeria, 2013. I was holding a series of outdoor crusades and went to rest in my hotel room with the founder of a Christian television network who traveled with me. We were praying for God's direction for the night as we worshiped the Lord in the room. The Holy Spirit directed me to these words in the third chapter of Acts.

Acts 3:1-9:

> Now Peter and John went up together into the temple at the hour of prayer, being the ninth hour. And a certain man lame from his mother's womb was carried, whom they laid daily at the gate of the temple which is called Beautiful, to ask alms of them that entered into the temple; Who seeing Peter and John about to go into the temple asked an alms. And Peter, fastening his eyes upon him with John, said, "Look on us." And he gave heed unto them, expecting to receive something of them. Then Peter said, "Silver and gold have I none; but such as I have give I thee: In the name of Jesus Christ of Nazareth rise up and walk." And he took him by

> the right hand, and lifted him up: and
> immediately his feet and ankle bones
> received strength. And he leaping up
> stood, and walked, and entered with them
> into the temple, walking, and leaping, and
> praising God. And all the people saw him
> walking and praising God...

There was a beggar at the gate called Beautiful. The beggar had been there his whole life begging for a living. Peter had the faith simply to believe the commission Jesus Christ gave him, after three and a half years of demonstration of this power. Jesus never told Peter this was intended only for him. As a matter of fact, Peter said something like, "I have been given this gift of the Spirit freely, and I give it to you freely." We still have a commission to give it freely.

We drove out to the venue where the meeting was taking place, and the Spirit started to stir during the worship time. I felt led to give an altar call for salvation, and hundreds responded. The TV founder prayed for an entire section to receive the baptism of the Holy Spirit. It was glorious. Before I started to preach this powerful message about the man at the gate in Acts 3, I asked everyone to take their seats. All the people at the altar sat down except for one man on the side sitting in a chair. I looked at the man and asked the pastor at the altar what was wrong with him. The pastor said he had a stroke and had not been able to walk or function for some time.

The spirit of fear hit me, and I heard a voice saying, "Your ministry will be ruined because you are going preach a message about this man's situation, and he is here and won't be healed." The voice of the enemy was so loud that I was stunned for a moment. Then all of a sudden, a holy boldness came upon me. The TV founder pulled out the camera and started to film. I told the crowd how the Holy Spirit had given me a message to share in the hotel, and I would share it with them. Then I preached my heart out. The camera had filmed my notes to show that I was not making this up.

The Holy Spirit empowered me, and before I knew it, I grabbed the man by the hand and declared, "In the name of Jesus Christ, stand up and walk." I took his hand and pulled him up, and the man walked across that stage twice. He had not walked at all before this. The people went crazy, applauding and praising God! The pastors started to magnify God, and miracles broke out among the people.

I love sharing about the time in Pakistan, 2015, that a blind child was brought up to a crusade; God healed him, and he saw his mother for the first time in his life! I can tell you about the time in Knoxville, Tennessee, when a man received his eyesight. I can tell you about the time in Brisbane, Australia, where a deaf ear opened up, and the pastor confirmed the healing. In Ghana, when a lady brought to a meeting on a stretcher ran home after her healing, or in Nigeria in 2009 when a softball-size tumor fell off a lady after getting her to rub it with anointing oil for a few minutes. Her husband accused us of using black magic, but I told him it was no magic but the healing power of Jesus Christ. Then he gave his life to Jesus.

I also love to share the story about Kebira slums in Nairobi, Kenya, the largest slum in the world, with over one million people living in it. In 2010, I took a team to hold the largest outdoor crusade WNIM had ever held. We set up a stage in the middle of the slum and rented a sound system that you could hear for miles. The smell of open sewage and death almost made me throw up, but I asked the Holy Spirit for strength. After five nights of awesome meetings, many salvations, healings, and deliverances, God did something miraculous. The slum drunk came forward, and my dear friend Billy Mayo prayed for him. He was instantly set free and in his sound mind, sober, praising God. The crowd went wild because they had known him for many years. He was the outcast in the city of outcasts, but now he was whole. That miracle set off a wave of healings and miracles released for the rest of the meeting. Billy also prayed for a man in a Warrior Nations Nigerian Crusade whose deaf ear popped open, and the village celebrated in loud praises because they knew he had been deaf from birth, yet that night he could hear!

Back at the Kenyan hotel, the ministry team was eating a meal to celebrate all the Lord had done that week. The host pastor came bursting in the hotel, begging me to go to Nairobi's main hospital. His assistant pastor was bleeding from his mouth, nose, and other places. The doctors told him they did not know what it was but that he would not make it through the night. I was so scared because it sounded like Ebola. The Holy Spirit said, "Go," and so I jumped into the car and went. For the entire car ride, the Holy Spirit told me I would be fine and not to be scared.

I walked into the hospital, which looked like a veterinary hospital, and people were lying on beds moaning and groaning. No rooms or special care existed. I walked up to the man whom we came to see. I prayed for him to be whole in the name of Jesus. He sat up in the bed. The blood dried up right there. I don't speak Swahili, but the Kenyans knew the presence of heaven. They all pointed to their foreheads for me to lay hands on them, and I did. The Holy Spirit healed some, and they went home healed.

In 2014, I was preaching a revival in my home city, Greenwood, South Carolina. A woman there could not speak normally. She had been unable to speak, even though she had been going to a speech therapist for years to gain her speech back. When she spoke, it sounded like a deaf person's speech. I thought she was deaf. Apparently, she had had this impediment to happen suddenly, and it had lasted for years, only now getting worse. She came to the second night of revival, came forward, and confessed by writing down on a piece of paper given to the pastor that she had been raped with a hammer by someone and held a giant burden of unforgiveness inside. She had held on to it for years, but she wanted to let it go this night. She did, and we—the Lord and the ministers there—broke the power of unforgiveness over her life. She went down on the floor, and an evil spirit battled with her for five minutes or so, and then she got up off the floor and went back to her seat. Thirty minutes later, she had a microphone in her hand declaring God's healing power in a full natural voice. Totally healed! She sang a special the next night. The power of the Holy Ghost broke out on the youth, and the revival was extended many nights, with many salvations, healings, and signs!

I have so many of these stories that I could write about them all, but the point is that you understand miracles are for today!

God says, "To another the working of miracles; to another prophecy; to another discerning of spirits…" (1 Corinthians 12:10)

Don't Be a Spiritual Nut, Be a Fruit

In August 1999, I was in Central America during the Costa Rican rainy season. One warm summer night, I was sleeping on a couch in a missionary compound in a small village called "Grand Del Ora" in the Mid-Southern part of the nation. The village of a few hundred people was strategically located on the side of a mountain range where the Bre Bre and the Ca Bre Indians lived.

I woke up at 3 a.m. to the presence of something I had never felt before. It was the supernatural power of love and holy fear of the Holy Spirit I had never experienced before. I looked up outside the window and saw an electric storm streaking across the sky. As I watched this awesome natural light show that spanned from one end of the skyline to the other, I heard a voice speak to me that I would later identify as the same voice that spoke to me during my "Damascus Road" salvation experience. It was the voice of the Holy Spirit of Jesus Christ.

The words He spoke to me would radically alter my life. What happened that night changed my character forever? I had spent eight years of my life being a hard gangster. I had beaten people up professionally, cheated people, and lied to people. I was completely self-centered and self-driven, but after this night, I would forever be a different man. I received revelation and an impartation of love. This is what the Lord said to me that night:

"If I created the most powerful weapon in the world, it would be a weapon that could harness the awesome power of love and inject it into the heart of the masses. It would be more powerful than all the weapons of mass destruction ever made. It would subdue the hearts of kings. Love is transcendental to life. The more love you have, the more love you will give. You can't give something you don't have.

"The problem with many people is they seek to find love from others first before they give it. You must sow before you reap. You must get love from the source of love first and then give it to each other. You cannot truly give something that you do not have.

"I believe this principle of love is the reason many marriages are failing. The couples have unmet expectations from an imperfect human rather than a perfect God. God alone can fill and satisfy. Love never fails! Even when love is tough, it still will not fail. Tough love is still love."

As these words burned into my heart, I wrote them down intently. I began to think on these words spoken to me on this divine summer August night. I began to realize that God had already created that weapon that injected love like this.

That weapon was Jesus Christ, and it was injected into us by the Holy Spirit! I believe the greatest move God will ever release in the realm called earth is a supernatural capacity to love the unlovable. To see a messed-up, burned-out human and love them as Jesus loves us. This unselfish love is the "greater works" Jesus referred to when He lived on earth. You and I, having a supernatural ability to see the best in people, believe in them, and have the unction of the Holy Ghost to impart that love to them.

John says, "Beloved, let us love one another: for love is of God; and everyone that loveth is born of God, and knoweth God. He that loveth not, knoweth not God. For God is love" (1 John 4:7-8).

A real danger exists in seeking after the supernatural power of God without having the supernatural love of God. For every gift of the Spirit that manifests, there should be a corresponding manifestation of the fruit of the Spirit. If this correlation doesn't take place, we see an imbalance in the supernatural realm. The Bible says you can cast out devils and still go to hell. It says you can prophesy to people, but without the fruit of love, you are just making a bunch of noise. The Bible says you will know them by their fruit, not their gifts.

Many will say to Me on that day, "Lord, Lord, did we not prophesy in Thy name, and in Thy name cast out demons, and in Thy name perform many miracles?" And then I will declare to them, "I never knew you; Depart from me, you who practice lawlessness."

Matthew 7:22-23

In 2005, I landed my very first opportunity to be on the TBN *Praise the Lord* program. The night before, the bishop that was hosting the show called me and told me to prepare the preaching portion of the program. I was so excited I couldn't sleep! I went into the prayer closet for a fresh word from the Holy Spirit. Later, as I arrived at the TBN location, I went into the room where the singer and the other guests were waiting. There, I met a man named Dr. Sidney Malone from Memphis, Tennessee. He made a statement that forever remained in my mind.

"Son, the anointing of the Holy Spirit will take you to a place, but it's the character you develop that will keep you there. The grace on your ministry is for an end-time purpose. You can operate in that grace for the work of the kingdom for a while, but if the personal integrity (fruit) isn't growing with your gifts, there's going to be trouble somewhere down the road."

God says:

> But the fruit of the Spirit is love, joy, peace, longsuffering, gentleness, goodness, faith, Meekness, temperance: against such there is no law. And they that are Christ's have crucified the flesh with the affections and lusts. If we live in the Spirit, let us also walk in the Spirit. Let us not be desirous of vain glory, provoking one another, envying one another.
>
> Galatians 5:22-26

The fruit of the Spirit is accessed by faith. It doesn't matter what is going on around you. If you learn how to tap into the fruit of the Spirit in the realm of the Spirit, you won't be moved by fear, despair, or tribulation. God's peace will keep you through the storms. God's love will anoint you to love those that speak against you and hate you. God's hope will empower you to believe when all hope around you has vanished. I believe that what the body of Christ needs in this hour is a "fruit" revival. We need to see believers sustained by the *fruit* of the Spirit, not just a manifestation of the *gifts* of the Spirit. That sustenance should make the church different from the world.

Contact Information

Interested in learning more? Would you like help implementing *Memoirs of the Miraculous* in your church?

Engage Shawn Patrick Williams to speak to your church, train, and work with your leaders to establish a revival culture.

Call the WNIM office in Greenwood, South Carolina, for more information at 864-227-0508.

You may also visit warriornations.org and send a request at info@warriornations.org.

Shawn Patrick Williams, D.D., Author

P.O. Box 2352

Greenwood, SC 29646

About the Author

Shawn Patrick Williams

After being radically saved from ten years of drug addiction and occult involvement through a Damascus Road experience in a bar, Shawn Patrick received a burning commission to evangelize the United States and the world. His style of preaching brings a revival culture to the body of Christ. He attended Christian Life School of Theology and received his master's from the Institute of Theology and Christian Therapy. Shawn Patrick has spent ten years working with over four thousand troubled teens in a clinical setting. He has worked with many teens struggling with the occult, suicide, cutting, gangs, drug addiction, and many more issues.

Shawn Patrick has also authored several books, which

have been covered by the 700 Club, TBN, Daystar, TCT, plus other nationally broadcast TV and radio networks. He has had many of his books in stores like Books-a-Million, Family Christian Bookstores, and Parable Bookstores. Shawn Patrick has co-hosted and written televisions scripts for five seasons of Roc House Cafe, a Christian music video show which airs internationally.

Recognized nationally and internationally as a man of God, Shawn Patrick passionately speaks each year through radio, TV, conferences, festivals, concerts, and churches. His personal experience of the power of the Holy Spirit, powerful deliverance from addiction and the occult, and his gangster background have aided in giving him a platform to speak to the next generation of believers. His passion is revival fire and seeing Christ saves lives. He has a Doctor of Divinity from Day Spring University, was ordained as a bishop in 2009, and is ordained with the IPHC. He then launched Warrior Nation International Fellowship, which is an apostolic network. He is also founder of the apostolic training centers called i3 based in Greenwood, South Carolina.

Endnotes

1 Strong, James. "Tŏpŏs," in *The New Strong's Exhaustive Concordance of the Bible*. Nashville, TN: Thomas Nelson, Inc., 1990.

2 Ryrie, Charles Caldwell. Leviticus Chapter 20, in *The Ryrie Study Bible*. *King James Version of the Bible*. Chicago, Illinois: Moody Press Chicago, 1976, 1978.

CPSIA information can be obtained
at www.ICGtesting.com
Printed in the USA
LVHW052352191121
703795LV00004B/7